KALEIDOSCOPIC WONDERFUL

Poetry and Writing by

Honey Novick

ISBN: 978-81-8253-868-9

First Edition: 2022
Rs. 200/-

Cyberwit.net
HIG 45 Kaushambi Kunj, Kalindipuram
Allahabad - 211011 (U.P.) India
http://www.cyberwit.net
Tel: +(91) 9415091004
E-mail: info@cyberwit.net

Contents

PART 1. UNDEFEATED RELEVANCE 7
IN A FEARFUL WORLD 8
IT TAKES A WILLOW TO ROOT
A GERANIUM (SOME/SUM ENCOUNTERS) 9
WHO? WHAT? HOW? 17
YOU GET WHAT YOU'RE READY TO GET 18
PUSSY WARRIOR 24
I LISTEN TO MORE THAN YOUR WORDS 25
AS A GIRL * (FOR YOKO ONO) 26
WAITING 28
ONTARIO – LAND OF 250,000 WATERWAYS 30
OH, KANATA 31
WHERE POETRY IS THE ROAD 36
MONARCH BUTTERFLY 37
MOOD TANGO 39
GINGER, THE MOON'S RADIANCE 40
DON'T HURRY, LOOK PRETTY 41
BLOOD/ART/WALLS/SECRETS 43
HOW? 44
87, WHAT'S IN A NUMBER? FOR GARY SNYDER 45
SPICES 46
I AM A ZING 52
ZEBRA 53
YOU DON'T CARE –
THE OPPOSITE OF LOVE – NEUTRALITY 54
WHITE SNOW DROPS FEATHERS 55
WHEN ALL IS SAID AND DONE, HOPE 56
WHAT GROWS IN THE SHADE? 57
VIOLET TEARS 59
VIBRANCY, VIVACITY, VIRTUOSITY 60
TOMATOES 61

THE OLD MAN'S JAZZ BAND SPEAK MUSIC 63
THE RAIN IN VAL DAVID 65
THE POWER OF LOVE 66
FOR YOCHEVED, A STALWART
LOVE, RECIPROCATED* 67
THE GODS MUST BE LAZY 72
TEARS INTO DIAMONDS 73
POETICS: THE UNLOCKING 74
BE CAREFUL WHAT YOU WISH FOR 77
TO THE TREECUTTERS 78
RESPLENDENT 79
SALMON ON THE HUMBER 81
YORKVILLE MEMORIES 82
SIR ANTHONY HOPKINS,
I DISAGREE WITH YOUR POWERFUL WORDS 86
OLDER WOMEN LEAD THE WAY 89
SUPERNATURALLY DIVINE 90
VOX FEMININA DIVINA, MY DIVINE FEMININE 92
LONELINESS 96
FROM NUBILE TO BELDAME 97
MIMI BOUGHT ME A FRENCH BERET 99
I STAND THEREFORE I MARCH 101
SEPTEMBER 2001, A TIME IN HISTORY, INDELIBLE 102
CALLING FORTH MY SISTERS 104
SILENCE 105
MISSISSAUGA ARROWHEADS FOUND 106
IF I COULD 107

Part 1. Undefeated Relevance

In A Fearful World

In a fearful world,
a smile
is an act of revolution.

It Takes a Willow to Root a Geranium (Some/sum Encounters)

I.
Refusing to root, a stubborn geranium
is cultivated with willow water.

Method: place willow slip or cutting in water till roots form.
Use willow water to hydrate stubborn geranium cutting.
It *will* root!

Willows are native to North America.
Geraniums are native to the Mediterranean Lands.

Like the stubborn geranium, I am of Middle Eastern heritage
born in Toronto's Mt. Sinai Hospital, Yorkville Avenue,
reared in the Bathurst and College neighbourhood
then a melt/ding multicultural pot of immigrants,
multi-generational people from the British Isles
and those native to this Land of the Mississaugas of the
New Credit First Nations.

Today, some/sum of all I encountered, nurtured, cared for me,
like the geranium fostered by the willow water.

II.
My father used to say, "You will always be a Jew, first"
when I argued that I am a Canadian first.
Today I would say I'm an idealist/humanist, first
a cultural product of a very rich Jewish tradition
but a Canadian by privilege.

Challah Bread, braided egg bread, was the Sabbath treat
eaten communally, a braid for you, a hunk for me
then use your portion to sop up and clean your plate.
At the Sabbath meal, a community is formed
sometimes in breaking bread and sometimes in sopping food juice
or sometimes just being there.

Some cobblestoned streets, clip-clopping horses hooves
announce the delivery of milk, bread and ice.
This was significant for me as my father was the last person
in the City of Toronto to deliver milk with a horse and wagon.
It also meant we would never starve
as my mother made very clear saying
"since we had food, we were not poor"
(an enlightened way of thinking).

Growing up on a downtown street after WWII
saw many immigrants welcomed with the promise
of great things to come and the disappointment
that gold-paved streets were a myth.
One of my earliest memories is the visitors to our home whose arms
usually covered, occasionally revealed tattooed numbers
before a quick cover-up and furtive glances to make sure
the little girl didn't see
but the little girl did see and was verbal enough to ask
"what was that?"
"THAT" for sure wasn't taught in any school I went to.

Another remembrance was of encountering immigrants
outside of ourselves, but somewhat looking like us,
Italians, who scooped poop left by the horses
used to fertilize homeland-brought tomato seeds
"a pinch of sugar is the secret ingredient to good sauce".

Italy's musical language caught my ear -
opera singing while digging through the ground to make subways-
"Va Pensiero" wafts, echoes,
overshadowed by a few neighbours killed in those subway tunnels
beautiful, hard-working men, tragic like the opera.

III.
One day there was a welcome party for a family who left Cuba
"Cuba" the mysterious hushed- toned word with huge meaning.
I was a child and didn't understand but never forgot that word
and that other word, "Fidel Castro"...always spoken in innuendo,
what *was* this language?

IV.
Protected by the "Talmud Torah", (a school for Torah Study)
I didn't have much experience outside my small world
until my parents rented a room to a 16 year old girl from
Glace Bay, Nova Scotia who listened to Hank Williams
constantly
she was nice to me and I loved the music until her presence
actualized what being Canadian means. Her father and brothers
were trapped in the mines in Glace Bay and my mother worked
tirelessly to make sandwiches for her to take home.
We weren't miners but we felt the dread of the dark mines.

Our neighbourhood welcomed Jewish refugees
of the Hungarian Revolution, every Jew had to participate/
I was assigned a duty – take the kids to school.
I didn't want to – they were dour
but I had to until they moved to what is now St. Jamestown,
brand new, just built. We went to the opening,
walked around empty clean smelling buildings and small apartments

a portend and initial birth of tenemental community housing.

V.

I was 8 or 9 years old and started rebelling.
I rebelled and railed. No more Talmud Torah.
I had to get out. I had to find creativity, diversity.
I hid in the closet and gave my mother a hard time.
It was no one's fault, really, it was
because the teachers could not explain to me
why, when the Hebrew Slaves left Egypt,
guided by Moses and led over the Red Sea
persecuted by Pharoah and his army
why did the horses have to drown?
I understood Pharoah's men drowning but what did the horses do?
No body could answer me and
I didn't want to stay where they couldn't teach me that!!!

There's a wonderful downtown Toronto school named for a British King,
King Edward Junior and Senior Public School.
They taught music and physical education.
They taught tolerance and I knew I was being tolerated,
dressing like Lorna Doone one day, someone else another.
In time they encouraged me to sing, to write, to dream
to be extraordinary!
Even at King Eddy, there was darkness, pain,
some gang mentality and girls who didn't read books,
however, it was at King Edward, a persistent music teacher implored
my mother to have me take private music lessons
eventually paving the road to the Royal Conservatory.
I couldn't rebel this time, I had to bargain,
I'll study and practise each day if mother agrees to the lessons,

a discipline that to this day serves me
(even though the standard was set by our
relative in-law Louis Applebaum
head of music at Stratford Shakespearean Festival).

It was at King Edward that I bore witness
to some mean kids sticking a "retarded" Chassidic
boy with thumb tacks and I started screaming to leave him alone.
This 9 year old Rebel with a Voice was choosing her battles!

VI.
Each day, each encounter brought a new lesson
a new challenge, a greater question of who am I?
Where do I belong? Why does it matter?

My father didn't speak much of his family.
As a baby, with a pogrom threatening Jews,
Grandfather Gershon Novick abandoned
his wife, Deborah, disabled daughter
(her name was never spoken) and son David
in Grodno, Belorus
to come to the Promised Land of Chicago, USA.
My mother's side of the family became "chalutzim" pioneers
to the other Promised Land - Palestine.
My father only considered himself
a sabra, cactus fruit metaphoric native from Palestine, Israel.

My mother's family were settlers and
indigenous to the middle east, Palestine.
Her father, Moshe, came from North Africa
spending his days learning the Jewish holy books
then married an aristocratic Austrian Jewish settler
and sired 9 children. My mother was No. 7.

They were poor. What did money have to do with anything?

Ethnically, I'm a mongrel.
Philosophically, I'm a flawed, multi-faceted diamond.

VII.
Canada was as affected by McCarthyism as were
the intellectuals, artists, idealists in the USA
and I bore witness to this.
In our downtown home, my parents' rented rooms and those rooms
became a haven, as each renter enriched me more than can be known.
During the McCarthy era, a family came to live with us.
The father, Joe, had been jailed for his Communist beliefs.
Upon release, the family needed a place to live
and they came to live with us,
not because we were communists but because they were Jews.
I was 3 or 4 and they meant more to me than my biological
family.
Not the mother, nor father, nor son nor daughter
ever talked down to me nor treated me other than a person.
They never used guile nor wiles to manipulate me,
didn't speak baby talk or try to hide anything.
Even though it was only the father who was imprisoned,
his family were in a different kind of prison, of stigma
but they all lived and walked in dignity.
This formed me and I howled when they moved away
not wanting to let Bella, the mother's feet be removed from my
hands.

Just like the willow water, nourishing the geranium,
each story enhanced me, bred me, helped me develop.

VIII.
When music would lead the way for my life's journey,

I volunteered at Mariposa Folk Festival,
being assigned to the "Native Section."
Picking up a brochure advertising Ojibway Language lessons – free,
I signed up but before the Native community got to know me,
I tried to find innovative ways of sharing my hometown.
When not performing, I took the Inuit Throat Singers on the Subway.
They were terrified. A cold August was too warm for them.
Through sign language and good intentions,
we muddled through and got along well.
I think it was because I was silent and observant.
The volunteer group did so well, we each were given a $25.00 bonus!

Ojibway classes were held at the now defunct Ontario Metis and Non-Status
Indian Association. The director, Jim, loved to play country music.
He asked if I could sing. I could sing country music. A folk singer
by any other name is still a folk singer. I was hired as a secretary
but was sent to sing on Reserves (Wikwemikong) and Prisons
under the Labour Initiative Program and a Prime Minister (P. Trudeau).
The friendships and lessons of that day hold to this day.
My sister friend Pauline (Cree Elder Pauline Shirt) reminds me
that I took the kids to art galleries and beach parties.
In time, she would imbue me with the meaning of smudging,
water-keeping and honouring the strawberries. This sacred knowledge,
as well as Yohrzeit, Jewish candles of remembrance, are some rituals that
I honour and practice.
Pauline and I have a special language memory.
Each bearing witness to a history and time

only we could know. A blood memory.
A Jew and a Cree, bonded in respect and time.

IX.
To be Canadian, to become Canadian...
these are questions. Sometimes this question wastes time.
In defining me, I define my life's journey.
My life's journey doesn't define me.

In caring for the rooted willow, I connect to the earth.
In watering a transplanted geranium, I am reminded
of impermanence and optimism –
almost the credo of the Wandering Jew.
I am reminded that it is a woman's place to keep the water.
In watching roots grow from this geranium, I see
possibilities. That is what it means to be a Canadian.
Possibilities and profound gratitude.

Who? What? How?

I'm gonna holler
I'm gonna yell
I'm gonna ask you, nicely, to tell
me a story about your name.

Your name is a story.
Your story is a name.
A story, your name,
would you like to play a game?

"Who?" asked the owl.
"What?" asked the duck.
"How" asked the wise man,
"did the hen learn to cluck?"

YOU GET WHAT YOU'RE READY TO GET

When people ask me what I do, I have a hard time explaining that I am a "song/poet". I can scat sing (vocalize and improvise). I can write lyrics and then sing them, usually unaccompanied, and at the same time. I can sing art song, lieder, chanson, semi-classical or folk music. So why is it important that I tell you? It's not. It's important that I define who I am because as I define myself, I am "re-inventing" myself and that is important. It's not enough that I say I'm a singer or vocalist or songwriter or poet. I am that and a car driver, a consumer, a daughter, a teacher, a yogi practitioner, politically aware woman, friend, and a lot of other things. It seems to miss the point or limit what I do when I say I am a vocalist.

When I was a little girl, in elementary school, grade 5, I was allowed to take piano lessons. A piano teacher was looking to teach new students. Three times the teacher came to my home to ask my mother's permission to teach me to play the piano. I really thought I wanted to learn the piano. My parents didn't want the expense. But, three time's a charm and my parents graciously, after a lot of lobbying on my part, promising to practice, cajoling, etc, acquiesced and allowed this woman to teach me, once a week. She did what she could, then I graduated to the community music school and eventually to the Royal Conservatory. This all happened when I was 9 years old. Diligently I practised and would have been more disciplined had my mother not sat near me, knitting, saying "you made a mistake". (Shades of Madam LaFarge). As I practised and made mistakes, my mother commented on each and every misplaced note. Soon I lost interest in playing piano. However, I did develop a love of singing.

We, the "Con Artists" (as my friends and I affectionately called the Royal Conservatory and her students), had to learn varying pieces of music. The first I had to learn was Verdi's "La Donna E Mobile" from the opera, "Rigoletto". When I asked what the words meant, I was told, "Woman is Fickle". Well, how do you explain "fickle" to a 9-year old? The words were translated to mean, "woman was deceitful". Since I didn't know any fickle women, I thought my time learning this kind of music would be limited. In looking back, I wish someone had noticed how important the words were for me. It would have been a clue to my love of words, poetry, and the mysterious spirit.

At 12, I read "The Diary of Anne Frank". It was one of my political awakenings, inspiring me so much that I kept a secret diary every day for 9 nine years without once missing a day. I think that should have been another clue. The alluring word passionately capturing my attention. (Eventually, excerpts from my teenage years were published, internationally, in FILE Magazine, a project of the performance art group GENERAL IDEA).

The next major influence was Bob Dylan's music. It was the words that engaged my imagination and held it at attention. (For the first time, ever, someone asked "How does it feel?") I was so inspired by Dylan's music that I began to write my own. Those pieces were kept in a big envelope in a box in a closet. At least they were until I read that the great poet, Irving Layton was poet–in-residence at York University. With titillating trepidation and a lot of planning, (like asking my girlfriend Sandy if she would come with me when he would critique my poems), I called Mr. Layton for an appointment.

It was springtime. Leaves were sprouting and reaching for the sun. Summer was winking over the horizon and I was tittering about having my private and intimate thoughts put on paper and exposed to a stranger who is a brilliant and famous man.

Professor Layton drove from the suburban university to my downtown apartment. He wanted no food or drink, just the poems. He sat at the kitchen table and read each page silently and then, rose, dramatically closed the folder, proclaiming, "My dear, these aren't poems, these are songs," and left!!!

I was devastated, crushed, silenced (but not for long). I put the poems in the envelope, inserted them protectively in the box and back in to the closet for years. Looking back, it was like building invisible, emotional scar tissue.

Singing, performing, and seeking the truth of my existence seemed to take over my life. While some of my friends were travelling, getting married or starting their own families, I became sickly. Technically, I had kidney disease. The real problem was that I felt that my body was imploding. If I didn't sing, and sing songs that were important to me, I felt that I was going to die. With time on my hands, I lay in bed, listening to my pulse beating or ocean sounds as my hand cupped my ear. The rhythm of my body was different than the beats of a metronome. My own body rhythm had it's own tempo. My friend Sandy had a baby boy and I would sing to him. I started to chant, "A kiss without a hug is like a donut without a hole". Slowly it came to me. "A donut without a hole is like a fish without a bowl and a fish without a bowl is no fish at all." The words, the songs, were re-energizing me and my spirit was a-borning. I was very hopeful. I had to be, I was still very sick.

I received a card with words that said something to the effect, "When all I wanted to do was sing, I was accorded the honour of living". At that point, I knew I was alive. But it wasn't enough.

As I grew older, I was pulled, magnetically, to the pen and paper. I didn't understand what was happening. I didn't want to keep a diary anymore. Been there, done that. (I had a couple of excerpts published in File Magazine). What I wanted to do was write things that were important to me. That meant POETRY. Because, being a poet was such a lofty aspiration, in my mind, I wanted to reach for the ideal. How do I climb that magical bean stalk?

And then the door opened. On an ordinary excursion to the library, posted on the community bulletin board at a local library was a flyer advertising a course in "Writing Out Loud". That seemingly ordinary event would profoundly change my life.

The workshop was free of charge and the description was alluring. The name of the workshop on the notice intrigued me. The name was "Writing Out Loud". Maybe it was the idea that writing could have sound or that I could sound off with writing. Nevertheless I was determined to go with an open mind and see what I could learn.

The workshop was located in an unfamiliar part of the city. The evening arrived and determinedly, I headed out. Sometimes you just have to take risks, like going into unknown places to get to other places.

I found the building but getting to the actual room seemed like going through a maze. Eventually, I found it. The room wasn't clearly marked and no one was there. Was this really going to happen? Eventually people started coming in. There were people in wheelchairs and new immigrants learning English as a Second Language and people who seemed mentally challenged. About 40 people showed up. The teacher, Linda Dawn Pettigrew was tall and elegant and sophisticated in spike-heeled shoes. Her lipstick, nail and toe polish matched. This was the beginning of the adventure.

I'm an accomplished singer. What was I doing here? I had written songs and lyrics and performed my original work at the Carnegie Recital Hall and was reviewed in the New York Times. What was I doing here? I was so scared of not knowing where I was that I started to panic.

The kind and insightful teacher, Linda Dawn, with a name meaning beautiful morning, put everyone at ease and excited about doing this work. Her background was in literacy and mine in creativity. We met half way.

Feeling as if on water-skis being pulled into uncharted waters, I had to develop skills using my ideas, opinions, hands, – writing poetry, articles, stories. I didn't understand the magnetic pull of this writing, but I was helpless to stop the flow.

First, the rules. Forget grammar and spelling. What? This is revolutionary. We were encouraged to not worry about mistakes. Just write. Then came the first exercise. Tell each other stories about our names.

That was easy. With my name "Honey", I had no difficulty. It is an anglicized version of an ancient Biblical name. That was the beginning of the odyssey. Our names. The next exercise was timed, one minute to write about shoes. We all wear them. What kind do we like or what kind wouldn't we wear?

There were other similar adventures. Write about what you see in photos. The coup de grace came with the four minute exercise in writing about a bird. I've enclosed it here.

RED BIRD
I think of myself as a red bird,
Soaring high in the sky.
Not a robin or a cardinal, but a spirit bird
Who travels between real worlds
And mythical worlds. It never sleeps.

It is a witness.
It has no friends, no enemies, no family.
It is a spirit voice
Who takes on the mantle of a red bird.
Once, my friend M. Joe, who is an artist,
Sent me a small painting
Of a red bird soaring beyond the clouds
Into the blue skies.

I will never know how he chose to paint
A red bird and associate that with me.

I sometimes wonder if I was
A First Nations person in a former life
And if that red bird is something
I remember from those times.

Next, we were invited to stand and read our writings out loud. My turn came and I delivered my words, literally shaking. There was silence. As I sat down, the whole room broke into applause. I burst into tears. I had been scared and overcome with fear. My imagination conjured up every negative thing that could happen. But none of it did. Instead, I was able to touch the hearts of the people in that room. It was a special moment. Maybe you had to be there. In time, Linda Dawn and I became good friends.

Since that time, I have been challenging myself to write daily. I write poetry, ideas, lyrics, stories, opinions and articles. With every piece of writing, I am peeling away the layers piece by piece of this onion of emotional scar tissue and replacing it with a broader, more profound voice and more rewarding quality of life.

Along the way, people and unseen forces appeared to direct my course. They all appeared just when I was ready to greet the message they were bringing.

I think the message for me was that somewhere between music and lyrics, I found my authenticity, my passion, my raison d'etre and I only got that when I was ready to get it.

Pussy Warrior

I sometimes think I am the most rejected,
dejected person on the planet.
I get depressed and very, very sad.
Then, like a kitten (or pussy warrior)
I go somewhere quiet and lick my wounds and
find somewhere deep within myself.
A little niggling spirit that says
"You've actually been protected, the time wasn't right.
It is more important to make a statement,
get yourself out there and keep fighting".

That's what my inner warrior says to me.
It is the time spent quiet licking my wounds that are the hardest
but nothing lasts forever.
Do NOT let defeat defeat you.
You are important and you do a wonderful job wherever you are
and
the fight is everyone's fight. Do it in the name of

__________________,

do it in the name of the nameless.
Just keep doing it.
You won't be sorry in the end and now is not the end

I Listen to More than Your Words

I don't just listen to your words
I watch your face
I stare into your eyes
I check out your body language
I hear your tone
I make note of your words
I hear what you don't say
I interpret your silences
Most importantly, I trust my intuition

As A Girl * (for Yoko Ono)

As a little girl, I was harmed by the pedophile living next door
He enticed all the little girls to come watch TV
TV was a phenomenon at that time
I was told not to tell because "good girls don't tell"
I didn't tell, I was a good girl, but the bad girl on the other side of the street told
Her mother called the police
my mother hit me for not telling her
and then telling me I will forget about this one day
I never have

As a girl I was taught to behave
ankles crossed, dress hem over the knees
don't get dirty
but I didn't cross my ankles, I wore pants
and I loved the feel of dirt on my hands

As a young woman with breasts developing
men and some women assumed they could touch me
without my permission
and I would be generous
I wasn't and became shrewish

As a buxom woman, conversations, quite often
were and still are
addressed to my chest
Once, a young man pulled my bra back strap
I turned and grabbed his privates
He left me alone after that

I am damaged but I am not broken
I am hopeful
I have risen from despair and found hope
I have gained strength and kindness
but I am resilient and caringful
I know I am different
I respect me and have found ways
to try to respect those who try to take me for granted
I am an ARISING WARRIOR, mouthy, smart
articulate, fun, trustworthy, kind
I am ARISING
I ar i sing

* In 2016, Yoko Ono sent out a call to women all over the world to participate in a show called "RISING". We were invited to take a photo of our eyes only, write a story about our "rising", write only our first names and our country on the bottom. Those selected would be placed on a wall at the Reykjavik Art Museum in Iceland. Mine was selected. This was my entry.

Waiting

waiting, I am forced to look, be observant
realize perspectives multi-faceted as a diamond
and as dazzling

waiting for the verdict from the grand jury
of a racially divided town
I pray
I pray and hope that the decision will make a difference
be uplifting
offer some semblance of humanity
instead of the same old, same old

this is not a new story, it just has a different cast and crew —
a young man, black, fatally shot by a white police officer
this is "Les Miserables" played out
but not as Jean Valjean

waiting for my recording to be mixed and mastered,
forced to weigh the pros and cons of being patient,
of understanding the deeper meaning of being tolerant
I want to scream and flail my arms. Waiting,
I have to imagine, use imagery
keep myself occupied

I choose to see myself as a pupa, a chrysalis
slowly, slowly metamorphosing
into a winged spirit
unfettered, unconstrained, unencumbered by others
where I become free to create my own destiny

waiting, I am drawn to make a difference
I want things to be different, good
bill wants things to be better.

in a busy world of turmoil and uncertainty
I can only master my small part
yet, this hope of seeing,
feeling a difference for the better,
is invigorating

waiting for bill (bissett) to go to a birthday celebration,
I hang my head in grateful appreciation.

Ontario – Land of 250,000 Waterways

land of 250,000 waterways, interconnected
living waterways pulsing, like blood in human veins
at times ice or steam
telling of ancient stories

listen to the wind, unfettered
ranting, swirling, blowing
from the Arctic tundra to the arable south
saying to the leaves "get off the trees
cover the ground"

relatives will be arriving
snowflakes, hail, icicles
reminding one and all
this earth is diverse

remember the lily of the forest
the trillium, precious as an orchid
remember the sweetness of maple sap
it will flow again

people appear like blades of grass
needing the waters of life
this land is yours, care for her

Oh, Kanata

Oh, Kanata my village, settlement, home on sacred land
I adore you
the soles of my feet tread your lushness
toes digging into your fertility
stones bearing memories of times unrecorded
waves singing sacred songs of invisible relatives

I.
A fallen leaf finds its place on the ground
as does a flyer advertising Ojibway language lessons
this flyer lies waiting for someone to take notice,
re-place or simply pick it up.
I am that person.

How wonderful to be given a serendipitous gift, like manna from heaven!

Thus I enrolled in Ojibway language class
taught by a woman, same as my very young age, fresh to the city
from Manitoulin Island's Wikwemikong Reserve.
I wanted to learn, listen, observe sounds
until cultures meld.

Child of Wanderers encounters Child of Earth Keepers
progress touched by hearts

II.
It is not always language that communicates.
Harsh lessons reveal character through bad behaviour

words broken, sincerity questioned.
Money, what is the value of money?
I give what I have
you take what you need
I take what I want
you keep what you need
do we care that money feeds us?
or is a spiritual communique?
or clothes us or keeps us warm?
Does it matter that money, as a power, is misused?

III.
Oh, Kanata my village, settlement, home on sacred land
I adore you
the soles of my feet tread your lushness
toes digging into your fertility
stones bearing memories of times unrecorded
waves singing sacred songs of invisible relatives

IV.
Each grain of sand and every pebble
witness history, obeisance, even rebellions.
They came, the settlers, the wanderers, the damned, the daring
and the darlings.
They came looking for refuge, they wanted redemption, caring.
Like waves of the ocean, people crested and landed
even species unknown, the land welcomed all.
Abundance was not a word, it just was
like food for all...
Can you foretell the storm?

V.
Once the waters raged and wolves offered warmth
once food grew just where we stood
once the earth sang songs in the breath of the wind
once the maps were uncharted, intuition gave the hint

Now the times have changed and water is a commodity
something to be bought, sold, branded, co-erced.
Wolves seek the night and a place to howl.
Food is grown on window panes, ergonomic and vertical.
The earth sings songs only the listeners can hear,
maps chart each inch while intuition gives way
to new languages of navigation,
this is where the brave must go.

VI.
There in the fashion and there in the food
there in the transportation and there in the "hood"
neighbours decide to live in peace, neighbours decide to fight
a division of rich and poor cuts through the traffic and clogs up
flight

A new Kanata, a settlers nesting, on scarred land ever sacred
the new Kanata, a village of many
oh Kanata, my home on sacred land
oh Kanata, for you, please take my hand

The space is crowded, blinded by the sight
strangers overwhelm in droves and drones
alacrity is hidden, as darkness overshadows the rill
yet in this place, a world of wonder exists.

This wonder lives in the mountains and soars in the clouds
it looks blue and sometimes gold, it looks odd
and vaguely familiar
it is a new world, once again uncharted
once again calling, a cri de couer
to the spirit of the voyageur.

VII

The land is settled, almost overrun, the people are not.
Here is the new Kanata, where nothing of true value can be bought.
Invisible moisture in the air nurtures the harvest,
soil composted and made alive, made new.
There is hope in a teardrop and love in a battle,
there is a reward for daring and here is the rub
a country evolves as its people revive
where dreams become manifest
dignity and respect, the target.

VIII

O Kanata, my home on sacred land
I reach out my hand and say ahni boozoo, tanzi, shalom , howdy doo
I am your citizen, a child of your girth
I sing your praises, I work in gratitude
O Kanata, here where dreams are given birth
O Kanata, thank you, merci, miigwetch, toda rabba, danke
O Kanata, hope lives in goodness and in stories and in mettle
hope is your promise and strength is your reward
Oh Kanata, my home on sacred land

Bama Pi*

* Bama Pi means "later" in Potawatomi, a Native American people of the Great Plains, upper Mississippi River and Western Great Lakes region. They traditionally speak the Potawatomi language, a member of the Algonquian family. Wikipedia

1. originally published in Canada's 150th Who We Are, Where We Are, Where We Need To Be Going edited by Bruce Kauffman, published by Artfest 2017, KIngston. Ontario

2. one of 10 winners, Calgary Spoken Word Society, Single Onion, Free Fall Magazine Nov 4, 2017

Where Poetry is The Road

Where Poetry is the road,
I am not alone.
Where poetry is the road,
I have hope.
When walking or meandering on poetry's road
I have friendly companionship.
I can ponder while slowly travelling
towards a world of my imagining.
I can body-surf through this fantastic reality
where I am benevolent and strong
I can wear leaves of shimmering stars
I can proffer a hand or raise an up-turned palm
Where poetry is the road
the roadway line eventually becomes a circle
and I am whole.

Monarch Butterfly

raging winds of turmoil
a colloidal vortex swirls, coils
impelling a need to travel

a swath of road
carved and paved into the Escarpment
offers a masterpiece created by a supreme artist
white Queen Anne's lace, blue cornflowers
yellow buttercups melding against a green backdrop

these wondrous blossoms
end at a garden of delight
flowering catnip co-habit
blue and purple morning glories
punctuate yellow black-eyed susans
accentuating purple salvia and Korean mint
vining green grapes and cedar
ascend the eternity of sky-high blue

somewhere a honey bee buzzes
mooing cattle low and laze
a cat flits between naps and lapping water
a breeze flutters above all, a kind of swaying temple

yet nowhere in this lush and beautiful paradise
is the king to be found
this is the first year not one Monarch Butterfly appears
a signal by its absence
there is more to be seen here than meets the eye.

the absence of the Monarch Butterfly
portends a message of great importance
Heed now, saying, "you've been warned
'The King Has Left The Building"

MOOD TANGO

let's dance a brazen tango
hip to hip 'cross pastures of green,
we'll throw caution to the wind
as we strut, flirt and preen.

a rose clutched in the teeth helps
when wanting to scream
at foolish greed, blind injustice
and people stupidly mean.

one step together in time
legs entwined in the same direction
keep moving, never stop,
unless looking for self-reflection.

Ginger, the Moon's Radiance

He was Ginger, the Moon's child
leaping from star to star
hair glowing like the root of his namesake

By day, the sun would bathe him in gold
a halo seen when the rays lit his mane

She was Auburn, the Sun's daughter
swimming in a radiance of a special landscape

By day, the Sun would protect her
casting an aura of brilliance down on her tresses

Some looked upon them as the unusual children
born of ethereal parents
others stigmatized them for being neither blond nor brunette
saying their differences belonged neither here nor there

Ginger, the moon's child didn't care
Auburn, the sun's daughter cared but was defiant.
She swung her locks, caught her father's rays
grasped them, like thunderbolts, and flung them
creating an arc of light

This glorious light cast a smile through the radiance
of a resplendent lustre shining out into the world
becoming experiences
others could only imagine

Don't Hurry, Look Pretty

I tell the face in the mirror,
"be happy
And if you can't be happy
Look pretty"

I don't know what happy is
I do know what lonely feels like
I do know what lovely looks like
............what melancholy tastes like
............where tunnel vision leads to

When looking left then right
Scanning the horizon, from side to side
I see a bigger picture

Once upon a time I made a vow
"to give thanks for beauty wherever I find it"

This vow may be a compromise
For I would always be grateful for my life

As long as I can feel the sun on my skin
Drink fresh water
Know my belly would be fed
Then I could laugh because laughter is the spice of life
I would appreciate my invaluable friends more and
Sleep in a luxuriant warm nest.

I know tears erupt like a dormant volcano
I know singing is a reason to live and
Romance is a temptation, a crap shoot.
I believe all this to be true
I love without expecting anything in return
Am satisfied that happiness,
When I make time to notice that
When I am not in too great a hurry,
And dress prettily,
I am even more happy!

Blood/Art/Walls/Secrets

there was blood on the wall at the St. Clair Subway Station
congealed, like dried up ketchup
blood on the wall at the St. Clair Subway station
a sight reminder
walls on the underground subway hold many secrets

there was a masterpiece hanging on the wall at the Art Gallery of Ontario
in front of a Chagall painting, a middle aged daughter asks her elderly
mother,
"Why did Chagall have to go to Paris?"
"He was a Jew, " the mother replied, " he fled to avoid persecution."
these art gallery walls, also, hold many secrets

How?

How do you do?
Tell me what's new?
How you gonna cope
when the leader's a dope?

How do you feel?
Tell me what's real?
How are tricks
in the world of stones and sticks?

How are you?
How did we make it through?
How hard is it to love
when you can't see the sky above?

Somewhere there is love
Somewhere flies the dove
Somewhere there's no why
just a flying pie in the sky.

How you gonna cope
When the leader is a dope?
Always ask how
can I bow to your wow?

That's the hardest bow of all!

87, what's in a number? For Gary Snyder

'...Nature is not a place to visit. It is home."
Gary Snyder

May the words you use as a missile, hit its mark, always!

May the vision you encounter be as clear tomorrow as it was yesterday

May the nature that you love and I love be protected and treasured and cherished, always!
Even if that means we have to redefine the meaning of "nature"

May your home and my home be built with the eternal strength of words, images, metaphors,
ideas, philosophy so that our home lasts forever and is passed down from one gentle spirit to another

May health be your treasure
May friendship be the mantle that cloaks whatever you wish to keep close to your heart

May these words from a friend not yet encountered give you the light of an outstretched hand

SPICES

A spoken-word performance piece
(steady beating of sacred drum)

(Wearing fringed deer skin clothes
Voice begins to speak)

Hear the beating of my drum
Feel the beating of my heart (repeat)

You followed your nose and found us
You claimed to discover us
We weren't lost

Hear the beating of the drum
See the crying of my tears
Hear the beating of the drum
Dry the crying of my tears

CINNAMON
CARDAMOM
CUMIN AND NUTMEG
GINGER and SAFFRON
TURMERIC
BLACK PEPPER
HOT CHILI

following your appetite
craving exotic flavours, you

caused the almost annihilation,
extinction of a people

the lure of the Oriental Spices
the fruit of a faraway land
enraptured you, captured you
until you sailed the boundless seas
in pursuit of this enticement, then
got lost and found us
WE WEREN'T LOST

CINNAMON
CARDAMOM
CUMIN AND NUTMEG
GINGER and SAFFRON
TURMERIC
BLACK PEPPER
HOT CHILI

the power of the spices
enticed you, reprised your longing
lured you, seduced you to
imbibe them, they'll
deprive you of your common senses

for love of the aroma
for want of the taste
the way of a people transformed
by the Goddess of Steam
who boiled and simmered
seethed and bubbled

alluring as a potion ready to take you
on a magic flying carpet ride

CINNAMON
CARDAMOM
CUMIN AND NUTMEG
GINGER and SAFFRON
TURMERIC
BLACK PEPPER
HOT CHILI

the spices tempted you,
kindled your desire
SET YOU ON FIRE
you needed more
wanted it all
stopped at nothing
not storms nor winds
not rains or scorching sun
the love of these tastes had you
impaled you to sail your ships
satiate your lips never feeling
all is well

hear the drum beat
it is pulsing, it is roaring
taste the flavours
lick it, savour

(Wearing kameez, salwar and head scarf)
The Great Siddharta tells the tale of the Rich Man and His Poor Son in the 2nd parable of the Lotus Sutra.

Not satisfied with his lot in life, a young man runs away from his father's house
he wanders from here and there and everywhere to no place
aging and growing in poverty

The father searched and searched for his child for many years and not finding him, settles in an unnamed city.

Even though the father is very rich, his wealth cannot buy him an heir
one day, the son passes this glorious homestead and is overwhelmed by
the magnificence of this mansion and flees from what it reminds him of

At the moment the son turns to flee once more into obscurity, the rich father recognizes his child. Elated, the father immediately wants to erase time and leave his vast fortune to the son. However, the father realizes his son is not ready to face his destiny and accept his responsibility, therefore, the father devises a plan to connect with his boy.
He sends two servants, dressed shabbily, but with a job offer of menial work, a job doing mindless cleaning, for a lot of money.

The son accepts this offer

The father decides to dress shabbily in order to connect with the son, trying to form a relationship

Like a frog in a vat of boiling water, not recognizing when the temperature or water depth has changed, the son begins to enjoy the work and take on more and more responsibility

Time passes, seasons change, view points differ

The old man becomes ill. It is the father's request, on his death bed, that this superintendent of property manage the whole estate. Upon acceptance of this request,
a change happens in the son. He becomes more confident and self assured

The father's days are numbered and it is his final wish that he tell the son the truth of their situation. The father believes his son is ready to accept his fate and destiny and understand the truth of his real identity, his authenticity

The father transfers his entire estate to his heir, his son and announces it is rightfully his

Hear the beating of my drum
You, traveller
you who are like this poor son
unhappy, seeking something outside of yourself
taking and usurping that which isn't yours
rather than owning and adhering to what is yours

in the name of the spices
you brought blankets with unseeable torture
and took our relative's skins to warm your bodies
you brought firewater and poisoned our water
you offered steel pipes with deadly sparks of fire
so that we could no longer defend what we honour
you took but you did not conquer
our spirit is alive, our songs are sung
our drums still beat, valiant, noble not in defeat

and all for love of the spices
CINNAMON
CARDAMOM
CUMIN AND NUTMEG
GINGER and SAFFRON
TURMERIC
BLACK PEPPER
HOT CHILI

I Am A Zing

I am a zing
I AM a zing
I am A zing
I am a ZING
I, amazing

zings are the light you see emanating from the centre of the sun

zings are the shadows appearing at the end of the day
they were there all along but they only showed up
when the sun went behind the horizon

zings are what you get when you pray for clarity
like looking in a microscope or opera glasses
adjusting them and then – zing, it's all clear
like hope after despairing pleas

zings are invisible messages winds bear
in waves and circles and breezes
they blow hot, cold, strong or gentle

I am a zing
I AM a zing
I am A zing
I am a ZING
I, amazing

ZEBRA

I wanted to be a zebra and wear stripes of black and white
I wanted to be a zebra but that just wouldn't be right
I'm a human being diverse in colours and taste
so being a zebra in stripes is a whimsical thought in haste

maybe I could imagine being a zebra roaming on the veldt
maybe I could imagine the freedom the zebra felt
maybe I could run faster than a hunters yen
maybe I could be the one admired by all men

People wearing stripes of black and contrasting white
are stigmatized by the image of some tragic plight
there is also the image of one in prison garb ensnared
dramatized by the zebra, the creature people loved and cared
I'd like to remember the wonderful zebra as roaming care free
when I wear stripes of black and white I feel that he is me

You Don't Care – The Opposite of Love – Neutrality

hate recognizes the act of betrayal
a promise of non-caring

neutrality is something different
it sees a person's dishonourable character
a behaviour that says "I Don't Care"
You don't care about me, about others
about the future you only care about
your own survival, like animals pouncing
on beauty, turning that into carrion

you are not a friend
you disdain community, people trying
to live harmoniously, like a family

the worst part is that you don't even know
your behaviour hurts others

your ignorance has nothing to do with education
and everything to do with sociopathy

and it's not even about liking you

it's seeing that you hurt others and
like neutrality, you don't care

White Snow Drops Feathers

white snow drops feathers
beautiful treacherous streets
unseen ice breaks bones

WHEN ALL IS SAID AND DONE, HOPE

When all is said and done
hope accompanies life's marathon.
When life seems like a veiled fog of delusion,
hope, like a seed, becomes germane.

Hope, a carved touchstone,
embedded with a message of light,
guides, steers the way
while willing the spirit
to never give up,
ever!!!

When indecision manifest
becomes the Y point in life,
confusion reigns at its hardiest.
Hope remembered, becomes
a beacon of everlasting light-hope,
essential.

Trust offers wisdom,
as the die is cast in the risky game of survival.
Hope grabbing your hand
swallows it in kindness
paving the way
to emerge as the optimal paean of life.

What Grows In The Shade?

What grows in the shade
without benefit of sun?

Shadows grow longer
when the day is done.
What else? I really can't say
I really don't know
If I plant a seed in the shade
will it grow?

If I plant a rock garden
would it grow?
Or would it suffer the erosion
of pelting rain and snow?

It seems there are laws at work here,
defying time, space and desire.
Seedlings can flow
and rocks do erode and expire.

What grows in the shade
without benefit of sun?

Shadows grow longer
when the day is done.
What else? I really can't say
I really don't know
If I plant a seed in the shade
will it grow?

If I plant a rock garden
would it grow?
Or would it suffer the erosion
of pelting rain and snow?

It seems there are laws at work here,
defying time, space and desire.
Seedlings can flow
and rocks do erode and expire.

Violet Tears

for Victor Braithwaite

Yesterday I cried violet tears.
Cascading like diamonds,
they fell into a champagne flute.
I then drank a toast to you.

Today I walk in green meadows,
grass blades tickling the soles of my feet.
Footsteps the only witness to my presence.

Tomorrow I will swim through
the pewter grey morning
recognizing neither colour nor shape
just the intention of the rain.

Vibrancy, Vivacity, Virtuosity

Vibrancy is the gauge used to see into me
like knowing where my heart's supposed to be
like reaching through the clouds and touching electricity
like waking up and feeling it's o.k. in the face of adversity

Vivacity is sometimes the place I want to live
a city within a city of mutual take and give
a place to restore what's taken from deep inside
a place where growth can be borne and love ad libbed

Virtuosity, another city of excellence in deeds
a place of time where focus is all that matters
where dreams are revealed and all is well
a place of carpeted paths and eager eyes

gauging a life of excellence decides the goal
where hands reach into skies and take hold
of energy and hope and structures in gold
telling tales of give and take, essence manifold

Tomatoes

they are a fruit and they are not orange,
but they are just as acidic.

tomatoes are varied
plump or plum or round or cherry
this is a lutein-giving fruit, FRUIT?
who calls a tomato a fruit?
Who calls women " tomato"?

a juicy ripe tomato with seeds
amenable to variable soil
like immigrants with seeds from home
sewn in hems
sailed over oceans
tossed on waves from continent to continent

re-planted

tasting of a home-land but
carrying demands and expectations

these seeds must grow nutritiously
for a whole new generation is offered
the savoured taste of a remembered culture

tomatoes breed seeds, and
like any revolutionary act
when seeds, like ideas, are planted
nurtured

cultivated to grow into
tomatoes, like a rise-up revolt
become true fruits of passion
love

THE OLD MAN'S JAZZ BAND SPEAK MUSIC

(inspired by Seymour Rabens, Chicago)

they speak music, continuously
for over forty-five years, they speak
the communal language of swing, big band
they are eighteen people, a tribe who
share a treasured language
this is the Old Man's Jazz Band
based in Chicago,/Evanston, Illinois

they comc together every second week
to play the traditional sounds of the swing band
they keep alive the spirit of
Benny, Harry, Bix, Stan, the Count, the Duke
names evoking white tuxedoes,
pink carnations in wide lapels
round framed eye-glasses, slick oiled hair,
zoot suits, watches dangling from chains
a style drawn, delineated, accepted
by a devoted group who speak music

They play for love, they play by sight-reading
(why not, they are all proficient professionals?)
they play to feel, they play and play and
play some more like devotees practising
a sacred ritual, a beloved religion
an anointed, exalted spiritualism, arms out-stretched
reaching out, fingers splayed, the hands of eternity

they play from an experience known by many
remembered by few

they speak a music of humanity,
crossing and uniting racial lines
they speak of a music born during historical segregation
they speak music contrasting and uplifting from daytime drudgery
they speak music and we start to listen, we sway
we move to its swing, we strut and nod and bounce
we hear the trombonists cheeks stretching,
expanding, gathering a gale force to send this music out,
the saxes and trumpets gather energy, erase time,
then we are the drummed and the strummed waking
to an elegance while a sleeping beast arises
from embouchure and breath
tapping toes, loosening shoulders, flying hair,
we join this swing music and enter
with it into a lexicon of inspirited poetry sung
crooned, hummed, cajoled,
tuned into a happening of the Old Man's Jazz Band

The Old Man's Jazz Band brings us an ageless gift
in a language that swings
then we swing, swing that thing called
SPEAK MUSIC

The Rain in Val David

(June, 2016)

La lluvia in Spanish means the rain
La lluvia in English sounds joyful

the rain in Nature's language
clears
cleans
sometimes depresses
always is welcomed
but not always wanted

The Power Of Love

The power of love, like breath,
is pervasive, unseen, necessary.

The power of love touches the essence of life force,
fuelling discipline, priorities, decisions.

The power of love is more than three little words.
It is the ammunition of energy.

The power of love, like food, sustains memory
harkened by solace
while keeping loneliness at bay.

The power of love, at times, appears as tears,
longings and a search for fulfillment.

The power of love is yours, mine and ours
as we are interconnected,
woven into each other's experience.

Even in the darkest night the stars' sparkle
confirms the pervasive power of love.

For Yocheved, A Stalwart Love, Reciprocated*

"…if you bungle raising your children,
I don't think whatever else you do
Matters very much…" Jackie Kennedy

In times of despair, I feel I'm the 'bunglee'
And blame my mother for being the 'bungler'.
When these dark clouds pass
I know this to be not true.

People loved my mother
And for very good reasons—
Her warmth, generousity, charm, and brightness.
She supported her friends,
And often didn't judge their character.
So, if you sold insurance, did plumbing,
Fixed electrical wires, were a butcher,
Sold chicken, eggs or Amway,
She would buy from you.
My father, the City of Toronto's last person
To deliver milk with a horse and wagon
Brought home milk, cheese and always the bread.

My mother and father loved each other.
That in itself is fortune beyond measure.
They became my "mother'n'father" (one word).

With her daughter, me,
My mother had a contentious relationship,

And relationship, indeed, we had –
Love/hate, guilt, co-dependence.
When I stood up to walk, at 9 months old, (she said),
I walked in the other direction from her,
But couldn't hasten to her bedside quickly enough
To be there for her as she lay dying!

I was the last of her seven pregnancies.
The others were either still-born,
Or severely handicapped and died in infancy.
I didn't know them and
She never mentioned them, ever!
(My Auntie Rosie told me much later).

Because I was born "perfect,"
Tacitly, much was expected of me—
I had to be the little girl my mother never was,
The toy doll she never owned,
The dream she fantasized would always come true.

In reality, I could do no right.
My marks were never high enough,
My opinions rarely agreed with hers,
My friends never good enough,
My personality and vocabulary too difficult,
And my looks never beautiful enough.
I grew up with a niggling feeling of "never enough,"
Something always lacking.

My mother and I yelled a lot, at one another.
Years later, as a singer, I was asked
About my vocal training and quipped,
"I had a domineering mother"

By 1950, my mother, Yocheved Horovitz:
— Survived World War I in a Palestine/British-mandated orphanage
(In charge of 2 younger siblings by her 7th birthday
the last 3 of their father's 27 children,
(depending on who tells this story))
— Had come to Canada on money her sister Leah
earned reading Tarot cards,
— became a clothes model in the Spadina Avenue factories
— lived out World War II, as a housewife, in Toronto
— financially helped to create the State of Israel
— had become Eva Novick, wife, homeowner and
after 13 years, a mother.

The 1950's were peachy pastel
Masking the looming, fearsome tentacles of McCarthyism.
My parents were able to buy a house
On Palmerston Avenue south of College Street
Where they would rent out rooms.
"Stay away from the window",
She would say to me at age four,
But I noticed and suspected something was awry.
Outside a black sedan with men sitting in it
Were waiting, doing nothing, all day.

A Communist (dirty, secret word) family
Rented these rooms.
The family needed a place to live
After the father, jailed for his beliefs,
Was released from prison
(background music Paul Robeson's "Ole Man River").
My mother insisted they live with us

Not because we were communists, (we weren't)
But because they, as we, were Jews.

Amidst this historical advent, we ate off
Colourful circles of Fiesta dinnerware,
cha-cha-ed to Xavier Cugat"s music
In the kitchen with the radio (no TV yet)
And sometimes wore mother-daughter
"Mexican"-style clothes,
(elasticized off the shoulder blouses).

By the 1950s, my mother was the first wave of women
Who bought into the philosophy of
"better living through chemistry."
It helped her cope.
It disconnected her from me,
Giving her authority to doctors
And pharmaceuticals (mama look a booboo).

Before she died, my mother
Heard me sing on national TV,
And commented, "Look at you.
Your whole life you've been nothing.
From nothing you became a somebody!"
I looked at her, stunned, hurt and retorted,
"I'm nothing!!!???
You're lucky I have a sense of humour."

Even though my mother has been gone a long time,
In many ways she is still with me,
For who and what I am is not singular.

Somewhere along the way, they,
My 'mother'n'father', instilled an invisible
Seed of gratitude that bore fruit
Resulting in my being able to write this tribute
As I look back with tenderness.

In the struggle to champion
My self-identity and self-respect,
I cope with the past by expressing
Appreciation to my parents for
Their stalwart love, unstinting in its depth.

In this environment, despair is dissipated
And I work towards a future with the sense that
"all things embody grace"
Maybe this sense came imbued
With the L'Chaim (to life) toast
Maybe this sense came from being the recipient
Of an undeniable structure of selfless love
Of all things expected, hoped for, of me.
I really don't know.
After all, the fairy tale promise
Of Disneyland's 'someday my prince will come'
(didn't happen), was just fanciful speculation.

I do, however, feel responsible
That the hopes and dreams of imperfect parents
Bestowed upon an imperfect child
Will manifest in a humanistic society
Prone to laugh, cry, forgive and
Evolve into a more compassionate, enlightened world.

*For the Canadian Museum of Immigration

The Gods Must be Lazy

the gods must be lazy
allowing style to trump content
allowing fear to roam free
influencing the mien of all
these lazy gods whimper and whisper
messages in the wind
and bask in the circular four seasonal changes
when there are more than four seasons,
and these seasons are dismissed, not acknowledged

the gods must be lazy
allowing the day to day activities
of humans run rampant
leading to starvation, greed, arrogance

this world has many that care deeply for others
homelessness and hunger are unnecessary as
Mother Planet is abundant and plentiful

it could only be explained that
the gods must be lazy

Tears Into Diamonds

Look… just over there
diamonds in the mist, sparkling everywhere

Every tear became a diamond
crystallized through pain and rain
Every setback moved us forward
leading to a brighter dawn

Unlock the shell
discover the pearl,
once a single grain of sand.

Climb toward the blossom, step on each thorn
Each thorn leads to a rose
the rose opens, petal by delicate petal
then perfumes all around

The storm has passed
all is nourished
each memory cherished
from thorn to the rose
from the grain to the nacre
there's a feast in every vision
there's a journey in each quest
there's friendship beyond the cloud-veils
LOOK, it is beckoning as it sails

Every pain, every grain, every thorn, every rose
see the sun as it grows
like tears becoming diamonds

Poetics: The Unlocking

adjusting my eyes to the same as it never was
unlocking the door, gingerly
stepping going forward into the new reality
the unlocking sometimes felt zoological
like an animal leaving its comfort
other times, like lolling in an immersion tank
knowing nothing lasts forever
other times it almost felt surreal
the almost normal expressed itself in poetic uttering
mine, Dylan's Cohen's, others

through these poetics I found my song
keening, breathing, intoning, humming,
chanting, vocalizing vocables
harmonic infusion of a soul daring to survive
surfing the cloaked waves of humanity, of faith
wounded, not decimated

the Ides of March, 2020, on the eve of the unprecedented Global Pandemic
not expecting it to last beyond two weeks
I didn't expect it would last and reshape the world as I knew it
forced to be vigilant in taking care of my mental,
my physical being,
my spirit

Slowly, invisible and sometimes manifestly visible
universal forces appeared
Roz on Vaughan Road telling me to go get food at The Stop on

St. Clair
my wonderful red Toyota "chariot" chauffeuring me to the lake
where rolling tides and the horizon comforted me
as if it were my own Mother's heartbeat

Mimi imploring me to come line-dancing on the street where:
Donna's approach to teaching, acceptance of everyone, gave insights into the
human condition and to my own body;
Ruthie J who came to sing Dylan's "Lay Down Your Weary Tune";
Ruthie J, Adam and Al sang with me in the park every week
as my fractured ankle healed;
Ruth S's constant encouragement as we wrote two books
"I'm Mad (I Matter, Making A Difference) and "Poemdemic"

the days of lockdown went on and on
forcing me to confront my loneliness, my alone-ness
while learning that victory favors those who forebear

Daily I looked in the mirror, seeing someone who looked like me
it was my own image, my aging visage
do I like her or not? My choice. No choice.

Like winning the lottery, I enrolled in a cooking program
where food, the great stabilizer, became the imperial metaphor.
With each recipe, every ingredient I learned thankfulness
"arigatai" as the Japanese say, meaning "welcome, gracious"

I held on to that thread of consciousness
pulled it as I would in a tug of war game
building my spirit muscles, keeping my humanity real
giving myself permission to "kvetch"

(Yiddish: to press, squeeze) complain,
then allow it to vanish

I looked for beauty and found it everywhere:
a turn of a phrase, the rising of the sun,
making my bed each and every morning,
the colours of nature and the sounds of the unseen
erecting a castle of hope with each find
getting rid of past hurts and misunderstandings
like my enslaved ancestors in Egypt building the Pyramids
I would survive believing
all would be remarkably beautiful
we would all imbibe enduring hope
pass it on,
one smile at a time

Be Careful What You Wish For

Be careful what you wish for
Wishes sometimes come true
It's the fear and terror of success
That could be haunting you

Success has responsibility
Attached to its name
Standing up, above the crowd
Means destiny, fortune and fame

The tallest poppy, like success,
Is a target 'cause of its beauty
Knives looming, cut it down
Life sacrificed in the line of duty

Be careful what you wish for
You just might get it
Love, happiness, friendship and trust
Come. Are you prepared to let it?

Be careful of expectations,
They ride on a carpet of surprise
Courage, strength, patience, persistence,
Blossom into your deepest allies

To The Treecutters

Please, please, please save that beautiful tree.
your breath will appreciate it as will your breathing
your eyes will thank you for recognizing the natural beauty
your heart will rest in ease as another living being was not cut down
as another living being was allowed to grow and give more than we can imagine

Resplendent

"resplendent" I heard this word spoken in an old black and white movie
and thought of you
it is another word that describes shining lucre, brilliance

you are my mirror image
beautiful, kind, seeking, raging, scared with paralytic terror
the paved way no longer serves
yet too meek to step off the pavement
onto unbeaten earth
I know the way forward is clear,
like forging a new path

i think of the past, a time when adventure was afoot
Quebec TV made an artistic film of Plato's "Symposium on Love"
I was a part of it, another being revelling in the splendours of life
the film premiered at a beautiful theatre in Montreal,
I went
a man approached me. it must have been my gold coloured kameez and salwar, saying "you are resplendent. I am involved with another but you shine and I wanted to give you something - a mixed-tape of music to make your life more joyous"
he couriered the music to me in Toronto
it was truly resplendent

I feel the moment, this ever appearing new moment
and feel sick to my stomach, nauseous, out of my depth

knowing I must challenge this invasion of my being
one that wants my ignorance to rule because it is easier,
more familiar, complacent
and thus I assail whatever gods carry courage as a gift
and entreat, implore, beg to be given courage as a walking stick
to prop me up, help me on my way
whether it is alone or with you

and I pray once again to hear the beating of your heart
to place my ear on your pecs and listen
getting into the rhythm that
transforms time and space
into one with the universal rhythm
I want to be the first one to step away
into the light of resplendent being

Salmon on the Humber

an act of futility
becomes
an act of amusement
this is the Salmon Run on the Humber River October 2020

September's rain was insufficient
the water on the river was low
the salmon swam their usual route to spawn
until they hit the weir,
a man-made concrete structure,
thus it was impossible for their route to be passable

yet the people came and oohed and aahed
with each failed jump
cameras bore witness to this wonderment
people and salmon in close proximity

classrooms of children came and oohed and aahed
at each and every jump especially with the thud
of the salmon on the concrete
I came twice and oohed at first
I want to believe the salmon will spawn
lay their eggs and die, as is their fate
giving testament and hope for next year's run

I want to believe that a skewered time
will find a way back
to a recognizable normalcy

I want to believe

Yorkville Memories

For Martin Robertson with appreciation
For Dona Levis who was there with me

Children of the Universe, come hear what I say
There's something special happening
On Yorkville, between Avenue and Bay.

There's gonna be a concert, we'll walk down memory lane
The music is free, the bands, something to see
So let's get acquainted with a little history.

Come to our concert, we need all the tokers we can get
Cause tokers are smokers fighting to make the herb 'legit'.

In the psychedelic colours of the groovy summer of love
Barefoot freaks'n chicks'n wannabes
Are hitching a ride to freedom on the wings of Peace's dove.

Back and forth on Yorkville, restless and inspired,
Up one side and down the other
Stroll long hairs, short hairs, rich and poor
Seemingly never tired.

On the streets of To-ron-to
Something deep was underway
Yorkville Avenue was the place where hippies came to play.

It was a sign of the times and the times missed the sign
Young people everywhere were starting to say

"No more war, peace on earth, plant flowers not bombs,
guns don't kill people, people kill people,
free love, ah yes, free love freeeeeeeeeee
Free clinics, free clothes, free food, free rent, free music, feel free,
Tune in, turn on, drop out."

If you listened very carefully, a mantra you would hear,
Young people's voices growing from a whisper to a roar to a tear.
"Get out of Vietnam and bring the troops back home
Cause nobody but a bunch of old men want that stupid war."
The message started with a drone, can you hear it still?
"Something's happening here, what it is is about free will.
Sergeant Pepper, whatta ya say? LBJ it's not okay.
Mr. Trudeau, what do you know?
I won't cut my hair no more, no more cause natural is beautiful."

Dylan said the times WERE changing and I could see it so
Rebel, hippie, maverick, all claims to fame, and we were all gung ho.
Identity, it meant a lot to me and everyone agreed,
If you couldn't see who you were, then how could you be?
A new nation is what we wanted where young voices would be heard;
But getting past the suits with short hair would patently be absurd

The movies saw the issues and played the freedom tune.
They told stories not heard before, nothing was immune.
Gangsters, outlaws, heroes, bucking authority,
The time was right for black and white love
To shock and awe society.
Black men and women rising, pride was in their voice

While women everywhere burned their bras proving there was choice.
Mentally challenged people finally came to the fore.
From out of dark closets, their abilities were explored.
With this new awareness society gained new girth,
While others sent their vibes back into the rich loam-filled earth.
Back to nature they would go to live off of the land
Growing beans and corn and peaches
While some joined an Indian band.
There was a revolution in everything and a far-out rush of hope
What exciting times they were like ascending a great slope.
What goes up must come down and many crashed on LSD
Amidst the surging throng, a whole new world came to be.

A message was a-borning. Could you heed its warning?
Love your body, love yourself, your neighbour and their dog, too.
Commune families growing round with hope and love and the
Multi-meaning "screw".
Many thought this revolt was spawned by middle-class youth,
But if you looked far enough, you'd find a deeper truth.

The dreams were real for one and all
But the dreams did not reveal
Food, shelter, peace, love and happiness.
Was it asking too much to feel?

On Yorkville Avenue, we would walk, back and forth and back again
Daily, nightly, on and on pausing only slightly
The ghosts of memories live and breathe
You can hear them in the wind…
Digger House (June Callwood's gift)
The mighty Gates of Cleve, the Riverboat, the Mynah Bird,

Reuben in the convenience store,
Did business with a joke or two and an open door.

Children of the Universe, let us start afresh
Those ideals must awaken, be pursued, like a worthy quest.

Those days are gone and some people, too
But the spirit never dies.
Let's catch it and start anew,
Keep those dreams alive.
Let's welcome the spirit of Yorkville
Wherever it arrives.

Sir Anthony Hopkins, I Disagree With Your Powerful Words

Sir Anthony Hopkins says, "Let go of the people who are not willing to love you. It is the hardest thing you'll ever have to do in your life and it'll be the most important thing. Stop giving your love to those who aren't ready to love you."

Yes, Sir Anthony, I will let go of the people who are not willing to love me.
I will list their names, say a prayer for them,
see them as the beauty of leaves falling from trees in Autumn
then I will just let go.

My generation of girls were never taught to love ourselves.
I came from a traditional family, nurtured to serve others,
marry and then bear children all the while, serve
like many warrior women,I wanted to sing on stage,
to survive, I did what it took to get by with dignity,
while keeping my dream simmering low
somewhere on the back burner.
Now I want to FLY as in First Love Yourself.

By loving myself first, flying, I'll take stock of my "stuff"
the clutter that brought me momentary comfort
while craving the gifts of learning, reflection and self development
until the self-realization I crave appears
I will fight feelings of desolation and helplessness
and become responsible.

If I want change, I have to find it within me
starting with perspective.

Sir Anthony, the most important thing
I have to do in my life is to keep on loving those
who aren't ready to love me. That way,
I will learn to love myself.
Although it is excruciatingly hard,
I will look for fun and expect it to speak to me
even from the invisible.

When the time is right, a lesson may appear in the form of
an exquisite person, one from time immemorial
he'll come but won't leave.

Although I may be terrified,
I acknowledge great power
I can't understand it nor explain it
so I call it love

With love I feel terror,
breathe in its power, until it empowers me
with life force and the courage of change —
it's either that or keep suffering

The Exquisite One came armed with a beautiful song
a poetic spirit
and depth

To love him, I would honour him and praise him and sing for him
and please him, or
I could let go and turn in a different direction
the daunting choice is mine
all lessons are repeated until finally learned

this work will be done by
discipline and honour – truth, reliability and forthgiving
acknowledging imperfections within me,
are like all flawed diamonds,
beautiful and valuable and the mark of character

I can't stop loving, Sir Anthony, because through love,
I gain a useful power
I earn a dignified spine
I speak with a smile and a nod
I develop the courage to make new friends
I learn to love without expecting anything in return

To keep on loving, Sir Anthony, is truly the hardest
most important thing
I will ever learn.

Older Women Lead The Way

Let's emphasize the fact that older women rule.
We always have,
as elders, wise women, foremothers, and

sometimes called witches
because of our insights, observations, sensitivities, and eloquence.

Finally, a curtain is being lifted.
The older woman is becoming visible,
she was always viable.
Our voices, as the curtain rises, rise with it.
Ready not only to take a bow, but to pave the way.

We are silent no more.
People are recognizing women as stewards of the earth.

Paper made from tree pulp,
reminds us that all living beings are connected.
That's why women are leading in the environmental issues.
Our sisters have our backs.
We will do what we can to help.

Women have been fighting, forebearing, for eternities.
We never give up.
We are resilient, courageous, friendly (usually), hopeful and
most importantly,
committed to make this world a better place for all of us.
We're in this together.
We walk the walk on the path paved
by older women as we follow those leading the way.

Supernaturally Divine

S exually
L iberated
U tterly
T heurgic*

It seems some things never change,
disappointing, but not strange.
For instance, take the war waged on women
for their bodies, eggs, yolks and albumen.

"You've come a long way, baby"
isn't far enough, I'm sad to say, because
fifty or so years after that slogan's launch
it seems we still haven't gotten up off our haunch

Women, stalwart warrior women
diligent, vigilant and true
no one will pave the way for you
realize, internalize, recognize
YOU are your own hard-won prize.

Earn a degree, get a certificate,
learn the value of the picket,
create a league or join a union
find out where to meet your legions
stand up tall, voice dissent
dream about becoming president

Humble huntress of the truth,
Embodiment of eternal youth,
Intrepid champions of the victory way
Tomorrow's success is seeded today!

*theurgic – divine or supernatural especially in human affairs

Vox Feminina Divina, My Divine Feminine

My Divine is found in humor
My Divine is found in adversity
My Divine is found in imperfection
My Divine is found in the desire for expectation, optimism, hope
My Divine is found in the Vox Feminina
My Divine is found in the reflection I see in the bathroom mirror
My Divine is found in you

My Divine is found in humor
like, the hopes and dreams of my parents
wanting a child reminiscent of Snow White,
until I drifted *
and then found my way, straight, down the middle, trustworthy
a loyal friend with the ability to honor humor
for it is in humor that the hard edges of life are rounded out

My Divine is found in adversity
every step of the way
barriers sprang up with words like "no, you can't,
you'll be rejected, don't do it,
you're too short, you're so smart, you're too old,
who do you think you are?"
And every step of the way
I found a way to surmount the walls,
the barbed words, the unexpected turn of events,
the snags in places other than my pantyhose
I had a faith in myself, a belief that

if life gives me shadows, make shadow soup -
easy as boiling water and waving a rock in the steam.
Delicious!!!

My Divine is found in Imperfection
for in Imperfection are the two words
"I'm Perfection"
and who's to say what's perfect anyhow?

I was the only surviving child born to parents
who faced six pregnancies, several babies
once referred to as "severely retarded"
all eventually dying
and when I came, they said, "she's perfect"
until I learned to speak, offering different opinions,
an articulate child, eventually silenced
for being insubordinate, mouthy, sassy,
too smart, incorrigible, and worst of all
WILFUL

But, in being wilful, I survived
I learned about priorities
I made a ton of mistakes and consoled myself
by saying "I'm damned if I do, and damned if I don't"
so I did
I persisted, I prevailed
I sometimes used humour.
I was more often than not, misunderstood.
When a local newspaper humour columnist was looking
for "Miss Right", I applied as "Miss Understood" and won!!
(not the columnist, a steak dinner, pre-vegetarianism days)

My Divine is found in optimism, an expectation, hope.
I have choice. To be or not to be, to do or not to do
damned if I do, and damned if I don't.
I choose hope, the struggle to see through the dark,
vaporizing pewter-coloured clouds.
I sail over and into the silver blue sky,
over barriers and with clenched teeth
like holding a rose of determination,
faith in myself that
if this is the hand that life dealt me,
I will prevail and be positive.
Nothing is worse than being dragged down
taking others with me.
No, I won't!

My Divine is found in the Vox Feminina.
My beloved father once quipped,
"who do you think you are, Shirley Temple, wanting to be on stage?"
"No, I'm not" I retorted, "because you're not Shirley Temple's father"
That is the Vox Feminina, able to defend without being offensive.
(unless necessary)
those thorns just bouncing off the invisible cuff of this Wonder Woman.
I sang, and spoke and wailed and keened and ululate.
I heard the song of birds in my voice
the roar of a lioness traversing her home-ground
the authentic reverberation of a woman's voice

My Divine is found in my mirror's reflection
morphing from familiar to unknown to

whoever I see. It is not smoke and mirrors
I am human art, definitely in the eye of the beholder.

My Divine is found in You
it is in you that I see me
it is for you that I say thank you
it is in you that I share courage and teamwork
it is for you that I write these words
it is with you that I walk this earth
and say "WOW" (Words of awesome Wonder)

Loneliness

a tribute to Mary Oliver based on a conversation with N.G.

he asked me about loneliness
mine, a mantle worn by an only child
his, a failure of a once familied man

yet my loneliness is where I paint the words
of my imagination
it allows me to hear the languages floating
in traffic, through the boughs of the trees
in electric wires, among people's voices
through hissing pipes
and gurgling toilet plumbing

what's loneliness?
we are never alone
we hear symphonies in thunder
we bear witness to species born and dying
we cleave to dreams unrealized and hopes to be found
we see the prophet's words come true
and feel the despair of the damned

loneliness, in the end
is never alone
we walk fast by ourselves
but we walk far together
who we walk with is determined
by the company we seek

From Nubile To Beldame

From nubile to beldame -
a journey, a lifetime, a thread of many words,
bearing descriptors like "bad girl, slut, wild animal, wilful
determined, survivor"
misfortune seeps through a hole
in the bottom of the bucket
chanting in a language only she could hear

She is prescient, knowing words create possibilities
she will boldly unleash a love for life
recognize beauty, learn lessons that
pause for strength, kindness,
she may teach you to express yourself as
she weaves love into a blanket, like a second skin
then wraps herself in it, laying on it, reshaping it
she knows time is fluent and time is fluid,
from precocious to precious
she accepts invitations from potential friends
befriends the unfamiliar
risks saying yes and no, knowing when each is appropriate
on her journey, she explores nature's spirit,
for this spirit moulds character and
aligns with the universal order of things

there is a law - cause and effect
when listening to silence it roars and deafens
seek curiousity, it leads to youthfulness
recognize the sound of your true voice, your strength
it will pave a path of sacred kindness

advocate for justice, deplore injustice and rail against it
observe those in agreement and those who aren't
abide and respect both yet be willing to be by yourself

who are your true tribesmen?
be helpful, share the road and ease the load
humility is born in asking for help
sing, laugh, draw, write, dance
make mistakes, they teach lessons through process
be a person of your word
make a promise, keep a promise, break a promise only
when absolutely necessary

know that time is only a fluid, mobile reality
it can be prescient, a reward

pause, move, enter, exit, look up, into, over and down
gain trust, find joy, seek wisdom
this is the true sound of surround sound
if and when possible, rest, become tacit
question and learn trust
always learn and teach in return

...these lessons were garnered from the journey's lifetime
they stand the test of time
they are written in sand
they sing in the wind
they travel in her being
they are her best friends
they are she
she brought them with her from nubile to beldame

Mimi Bought Me A French Beret

The Talmud teaches..."Do not be daunted by the enormity of the world's grief. Do justly, now. Love mercy, now. Walk humbly, now. You are not obligated to complete the work, but neither are you free to abandon it."

on her last trip to Paris, Mimi bought me a black French beret
I collect berets, woollen, warm, covering my ears
berets produce heat as it comforts and protects my head
it is cold in Toronto's winter

on Friday the 13th of November, 2015
people were slaughtered in Paris
at a concert, in a restaurant, outside a sporting event
the world mourned with Parisiennes
my French beret took on a new meaning
with its Eiffel Tower logo embroidered in red, white and blue
le drapeau de France
les couleurs de France
Lest we forget so quickly after Remembrance Day

while driving through the Escarpment the radio plays
"Sealed With A Kiss", a good song of the early 1960s
is it a remembrance of a gentler time?
JFK was still alive in the White House
the Beatles hadn't yet conquered the zeitgeist of America
Castro was rebuilding Cuba
war raged in Viet Nam
nuclear bombs were blasting in the USSR and the USA
a slow and growing rift was widening between generations

racist behaviours were slowly percolating
culminating in the Civil Rights Movement
while "Sealed With A Kiss" suggests what all young people hope for
a promise, a deal sealed with a kiss

not a handshake, nor a written contract but a hope signed lip to lip

In Paris, today, people are scarred and scared
just like in Kenya and Beirut and Mississauga
while a drought is slowly killing people in Ontario's northland

Black men are still hunted
gay people are still ostracized
women are still chanting for equality
anger, stupidity, festoons everywhere
while I gingerly walk the tightrope of survival
acknowledge the suffering of others
respectfully bearing my own grief
as I wear a French beret, hum "Sealed With A Kiss",
while I walk humbly, love graciously and pray for justice

I Stand Therefore I March

I stand for decency and civility.
I stand for human beings being kind to one another.
I stand for the right to speak up and out.
I stand for inclusion.
I stand for tomorrow and hope.
I stand therefore I march.

September 2001, a Time in History, Indelible

The dust settled
the air, more breathable
yet, the anxiety palpable
December, 2001
leaving upstate New York on Amtrak
heading south-east for the Big Apple
everyone's eyes darting everywhere
these were my impressions on the train

I came to perform at the 4th St. Church, Christmastime
I came to sing, I came to see and be
part of a time in history, indelible

energies were heightened, I was inspired
by the woman who shook constantly,
memories and experiences too new,
yet she had the courage to come
to the People's Voice Cafe, my concert
saying she was scared all the time
and the woman who changed her identity
by buying a Cleopatra-style wig
defiant, she would not cower to fear
nor the older man with the golden voice who
sang of 15th century Spain, "Adio Querido:
(trans. Goodbye My, Dear)
the time of the Inquisition
a time, perhaps, not too different.
I was especially warmed by the Pastor whose faith shone
as he welcomed singers, poets, visionaries to the manse

deflecting more serious matters as
he gave all of us books, children's books,
yet giving me the greatest gift, a long warm hug

what was once the World Trade Centre was now a hole
a portal of what is from what it once was
there wafting on the wind was a melody
a Yiddish folksong of the Holocaust "Zog Nit Keynmol"
"Never Say This is The End" as sung by
the great basso, Paul Robeson. This song, it's daunting rhythm
helped focus me as I forged friendships. That was my
survival tactic. Reach out, be a friend, or at least try to be one
as Ray Korona, he who invited me to come, said. Experience
NYC anew

Ray Korona, a beam shining from the crown of his compassion
soldered a warmth much needed

it is in this moment that the future is built,
why not create a beam shining from eye to eye,
heart to heart,
outstretched hand to outstretched hand?
and with palms pressed together,
I say "Never Say This is the End".

Calling Forth My Sisters

(written in a group taught by Westwind Evening)

they appear as four
in reality, they are one and the same
each a gift of strength, companionship and hope

when I am ready to "give up", Sister Nurturing yells
"what's the matter with you, are you a coward, ready to give up?"
I laugh and say, "yes, this reality is too hard"
Sister Nurturing morphs into Sister Humour
ready to tickle me with a feather before the winds
turn her into Sister Truth
she becomes serious, "hang in there" she caresses
"a true Warrior Woman learns forebearance,
like forging steel from a hot fire"

I am arrogant enough to want to choose my battles
Sister Truth smiles and says, "yes, it is possible
but life lessons are given to you.
Everyone will receive something, IF and ONLY WHEN
they are wise enough to receive"

after much silence, she swirls and twirls with the winds
then leaves
becoming Sister Spirit, She Who Loves
this is the goal
She Who Loves MUST
love even that which is difficult
this is the route to the light

Silence

Silence. The importance of silence is revealed
to singers and other musicians through listening.
Sit in a chair with feet flat on the floor,
lower back touching the chair.
Make sure the spine is straight.
Just listen for a minimum of thirty seconds.
This is not a meditation.
This is active listening.
It is the basis of all music.
It is how Beethoven was able to compose while being deaf.
Active listening tunes our ears to focus on silence or sound.
Become aware of all that you "observe" with your ears.
Especially if it is "nothing".
Some people in big cities are aware of the cadences of traffic.
In the country it could be the clatter of birdsong.
In stillness it could be the pulsation of blood
flowing through the veins.
Active listening is a true exercise.

Mississauga Arrowheads Found

5:00 a.m. Sunday morning, summertime
2 fathers, 3 children drove west into a rising sun
stillness
on the shoreline they walked, explored
2 boys, 1 girl
the girl waded into the lake waters
bare feet punctured by stone object attached to wood
she grasped into the sandy water and pulled out an arrowhead

she knew immediately it was important
for in her hand she held history

the boys were curious and wanted to see
she let them touch then hold her treasure
they gaped and pronounced it useless
threw it far back into the lake
never again to be recovered

heartbroken, the girl bent her head
looked for the history only a moment before held in the palm of her hand
if she could not take the evidence back
she vowed she would carry the importance of what will always be

If I Could

"My wish is to eradicate misery from the face of this earth."
2nd Soka Gakkai International* President Josei Toda

If I could I would, eradicate misery from the face of this earth
I would start with myself
I would challenge my darkness, the place where misery dwells
I would dare to go there and confront this demon
I would double over in pain
I would overcome this and stand tall
I would do all of this for my own sake
Happiness begins with me
you can have it as well, but only if you want it
a lot of people don't
they say Happiness is overrated
I wouldn't know

* Soka Gakkai International is the Society for the Creation of Value

www.ingramcontent.com/pod-product-compliance
Lightning Source LLC
LaVergne TN
LVHW091605170726
843492LV00007B/2261

* 9 7 8 8 1 8 2 5 3 8 6 8 9 *